Every Nurse's Business

The role of marketing in service delivery

Every Nurse's Business

The role of marketing in service delivery

Sandra Jowett

Published by
King's Fund Publishing
11–13 Cavendish Square
London W1M 0AN

© King's Fund 1996

First published 1996

ISBN 1 85717 119 5

A CIP catalogue record for this book is available from the British Library

Distributed by Bournemouth English Book Centre (BEBC)
PO Box 1496
Poole
Dorset
BH12 3YD
Tel: 0800 262260
Fax: 0800 262266

Origination by Trigon, Beckenham, Kent
Printed and bound in Great Britain by Galliard Printers Ltd, Great Yarmouth

Cover photograph: John Price Studios/Telegraph Colour Library

Contents

Foreword

As the shape of health care services is rapidly changing in response to a wide variety of different factors, new opportunities are arising for nurses and nursing to develop and expand the contribution that they make to patient and client care. Within this context, there is a growing need for clinical leaders not only to develop their clinical skills but also to find their way around the complex market arena in order to express to others the rationale behind their services and the impact it has on patient and client care.

The principle of marketing their services is new to many nurses, midwives, and health visitors, as is the range of skills required to compete for resources and having to account for their use in professional and business terms. However, it is vital that such skills are learned if we wish to play a full role alongside medical and other colleagues within both provider and purchaser settings, in shaping the type of care which will be offered in the future.

Recognising these needs, the Department of Health commissioned this work which offers both factual information about the structure of commissioner- and provider-units within the health service, and very practical examples from the experience of a number of clinical leaders about the influence of market forces on their day-to-day lives. Positive actions which they have been able to take to ensure the services they offer are well represented in business plans have been included and the new language of marketing is made clear.

My thanks go to Dr Sandra Jowett for researching and preparing the text supported by Professor Sally Redfern and Barbara Vaughan, whose experience of facilitating and evaluating the Nursing Development Units programme has been drawn on in developing the work.

I am delighted to support this publication which, I have no doubt, will prove to be a valuable resource in helping nurses, midwives and health visitors, whatever their setting or speciality, to ensure that the services they offer are made explicit to others and are well represented in business plans of the future.

Yvonne Moores
Chief Nursing Officer/Director of Nursing

Acknowledgements

Considerable thanks are due to the people who attended the focus group that formed the basis for this report. They talked fully about their experiences of marketing and of the potential of this feature of their work. The comments received from them on the draft report are appreciated. Thanks are also due to the senior managers who identified key points for exploration in the group when they were contacted by telephone during the early stages of this work.

I am also very grateful to Barbara Vaughan from the King's Fund and Professor Sally Redfern from King's College, University of London for their invaluable support at every stage of this work. Barbara Vaughan also attended the focus group, contributing her considerable knowledge of the issues to the discussion.

This work was undertaken when I was employed at the National Foundation for Educational Research and I would like to thank Dr Judy Bradley for her encouragement and for the very helpful comments and suggestions made on the draft report.

The funding received from the Department of Health is gratefully acknowledged, as is the guidance and assistance received from Professor Veronica Bishop and Pat Cantrill.

Dr Sandra Jowett
Associate Director
Public Attitude Surveys
High Wycombe

Introduction

Aims of this report

This report has been written for practitioners who would like to consider how marketing, particularly in the context of the purchaser–provider system, might be relevant to their work. Drawing on the views and working practices of experienced nurses it seeks to clarify some of the issues around marketing and purchasing[1] in a way that will be helpful to practitioners. Appendices 1, 2 and 3 contain some of the relevant background information about the climate within which marketing may take place. There is information in this report for nurses who want to:

- play a more active role in the purchasing process;
- work pro-actively within a multi-professional forum;
- reflect on how nursing can be marketed effectively.

A recent government publication (GB DOH, 1993) emphasises that purchasers need to know about good practice to ensure that it is more widely adopted. Interestingly, the report highlights that very few purchasers know of the good practice for which their providers have been singled out. It details a range of activities demonstrating 'the potential of nurses, midwives and health visitors to take the initiative in identifying gaps in service provision whether or not they are specifically nursing-related'. Similarly, Bryant (1993) notes 'the dramatic absence from the purchasing literature of references to nursing, particularly in respect of descriptive accounts of what is being done' and stresses the need to write about what nurses *are* doing, to stimulate discussion. The current report seeks to shed light on how practitioners can:

- identify gaps in provision;
- operationalise their 'good ideas' for developing practice;
- stimulate awareness and discussion of the structures in which they work.

---

1. The word 'purchasing' appears throughout this report because it is so widely used to mean commissioning, that not to use it could be misleading.

Study design

The main source of data for this study was a focus group undertaken at the King's Fund in March 1996. Focus groups are a well-established qualitative research method used to investigate participants' perceptions of defined areas of interest (*Nyamathii and Schuler, 1990*). They are a valuable tool in the search for a systematic understanding of everyday experience. Experienced practitioners, mainly clinical leaders from Nursing, Midwifery, and Health Visiting Development Units (NDUs), were invited to the group to discuss marketing and purchasing. Most of the examples from practice displayed in boxes in this report emerged during this group discussion. Further details of the approach taken are provided in Appendix 4 and the focus group members are listed in Appendix 5.

Marketing – issues and strategies

Why marketing is relevant to practice

Participants in the focus group felt that there had been considerable changes in the attitudes and perceptions of nurses in the last two or three years in relation to marketing. There was much greater awareness of how nursing fits into the 'business' approach of the NHS. The point was made very strongly that, given the current climate of change, it is important for *all* health care staff to be aware of the decision-making and priority setting that is taking place and that nurses need to make their voice heard. If this does not happen, changes will be made without the perspective of the largest work-force in the NHS.

As Marsh and Macalpine (1995) suggest:

> There is a need for awareness of the scope and strengths of the nursing role and practice, as well as the confidence to use that awareness in working for change with the other shareholders, who often have quite limited perceptions of the role of nurses in the organisational setting.

In the same vein, Adirondach and MacFarlane (1990) explain that:

> Sensible organisations are those which are taking action now to ensure they can take advantage of the contract culture, without jeopardising their current activities or losing sight of their objective.

The case to be made here is that marketing is relevant to practitioners because it underpins daily working practices – even at the level of when to discharge a patient – and provides a route for them to develop their practice. Marketing, as described here, broadens the nurse's role and encourages professional development.

Marketing in this context can mean:

- finding a niche for a 'good idea' for extending practice or being innovative;
- knowing where these 'good ideas' could fit into the system;
- meeting people's right to know – otherwise users may be unaware of a service from which they could benefit;
- the development of reflective practice as a means of clarifying what is being 'sold';
- celebrating achievements;

- adopting a strategic approach to achieving service improvement;
- encouraging nurses to feel good about their work and about saying so in public;
- turning the one-way channel of information (from practitioners upwards) into part of a genuine dialogue;
- writing effective action plans by knowing how your work fits into organisational structures and procedures;
- an examination of ethical practices and dilemmas as staff consider more fully how they should respond to situations.

Involvement in decision-making

A recent report (GB. NHSE, 1994) outlines a strategy for the development of purchasing, which represents 'a significant step towards a primary care-led NHS, in which decisions about the purchasing and provision of health care are taken as close to patients as possible'. Nurses are potentially able to exert an influence on decision-making at various levels. In the example in Box 1, community nurses are seeking to have an impact at the practical level of service delivery and at a philosophical level of service development. They are 'selling' their service to GPs, focusing on the skill mix required for the work and the optimum ways to develop provision.

Box 1

A locality manager for community health services outlined two key ways in which she and her colleagues needed to influence purchasers – one concerning practice and one the whole service approach.

◆ To move away from using number of patient *contacts* as the measure of service delivery. Much more sophisticated recording systems are needed to reflect accurately the wide range of activities community nurses undertake with patients.

◆ To emphasise the breadth and scope of the public health role community nurses could play.

More specifically, the example in Box 2, raised by a member of the focus group, highlighted how the nurse's day-to-day professional judgements – this time relating to an 85-year-old patient – need to be set in a broader context. One option here would be to 'protect' junior colleagues by not discussing this wider context with them. The issue then is the extent to which senior personnel should facilitate a working environment where all staff are aware of the background to decision-making. A balance needs to be struck between putting staff in situations where they could feel compromised and not giving them the possibly empowering information that they might wish to utilise.

Box 2

There were concerns on a cardiology ward about when an elderly patient should be discharged. He had responded well to the treatment he had received, but nurses were undecided about whether he should go home or whether the beneficial effects of extending his stay slightly would reap rewards in the long-term. The ward manager's decision-making was informed by an understanding of the need to justify patient throughput figures and other performance indicators. They provided the context for professional judgements about patient care, although not all her nursing colleagues were aware of the complexity of the decision-making process in which she was involved.

As nursing's working practices and roles change and develop, the opportunities for playing a fuller role in decision-making and service development will increase. Group participants outlined several ways (see Box 3) in which changes in their practice had strengthened these possibilities. One practitioner explained how GPs were now liaising with her and her colleagues far more regularly and were expecting to discuss discharges from hospital and after-care with them. This responsiveness to the nurse-led service emphasised how roles could be adapted. Five years ago, the current lines of responsibility and contact would have seemed unrealistic.

Box 3

Examples of nurses' changing role that may impact on their contact with others:

◆   nurse-led services;

◆   enhanced work in rehabilitation;

◆   expertise in working with people with eating disorders;

◆   developments in treating cancers;

◆   programmes for self-medication.

'Good ideas'

Another illustration of the way in which marketing has a practical significance for practitioners relates to how to deal with ideas for extending practice. Without an awareness of how they could 'market' developments, or indeed how they could be incorporated into policy-making, nurses may not go beyond the 'good idea' stage. The examples in Boxes 4 and 5 show how practitioners were able to move patient care forward by working with the system in which they operated.

Box 4

Nurses working in a [nurse-led] children's out-patient department were concerned about the number of children they were seeing who suffered from enuresis. The establishment of a nurse-led clinic specialising in this difficulty has proved to be a great success. Initial concerns about the appropriateness of nurses managing this service had been overcome and the clinic was thriving with a list of 70 or so children.

Box 5

Staff on an oncology ward were keen to develop their knowledge of ways in which the ill-effects of treatments could be dealt with as part of their service to patients. They found evidence that massage could be used therapeutically to good effect following radiotherapy, and nurses were able to attend training courses on this technique. By identifying this need, developing skills to enhance their practice, and making the case for offering this service, the nurses were able to secure funding for 20 hours of staff time per week to offer massage to patients.

What marketing is – and is not

In identifying how marketing can be an effective part of nurses' working practice, it is important to explore its many and varied facets. Patient satisfaction is one key feature. As the example in Box 6 illustrates, one spin-off of best practice is that 'consumer' satisfaction (in this case of a relative) may result in some rather unexpected marketing, and indeed may generate a network of 'supporters'.

Box 6

A terminally ill patient was admitted to a ward for elderly people, following a series of admissions to other areas. At this difficult and emotional time, his wife had been unhappy with his previous placements and had not formed constructive relationships with hospital staff. Being aware of these difficulties, staff in this ward, where the patient subsequently died, worked extremely hard to forge links with his family and were able to establish a mutual understanding. The patient's wife appreciated this effort at such a critical time, and she became an 'ambassador' for the ward, 'publicising' the quality of care she and her late husband had received throughout the local community. Staff were delighted that their ability to provide such support, in difficult circumstances, had had this wider impact on how their unit was viewed. Such consumer satisfaction was a powerful tool in their development of a marketing strategy for their work.

Some key characteristics (and some misunderstandings) in relation to marketing are presented in Box 7 on page 8. The purpose of these lists is to spell out how marketing can simply mean what many nurses are doing or developing anyway, namely evaluating their work so that it can be undertaken more effectively.

Communicating effectively

There is considerable scope for nurses to reflect on their practice and identify who needs to know what about their work. Having identified the target groups, the challenge then is to develop effective forms of communication. Bryant (1993) suggests that 'purchasing needs people who can listen to and speak several health languages' and that nurses are ideally placed to do this.

Effective communication has two main components, and these are outlined in Box 8 on page 9. The first is how language is used to describe something in an intelligible way to a range of audiences and the second is how appropriate terms are used to encourage understanding. These points apply to both written and spoken words. Information leaflets, for example, may be introduced with the best of intentions and

Box 7 – Marketing

WHAT IT IS	WHAT IT IS NOT
• Identifying, anticipating, fulfilling, 'customer' needs	• Something only the commercial sector needs to consider
• Acknowledging, recording and publicising strengths and successes	
• Establishing professional office practice for everyday activities such as answering the telephone and dealing with queries	• A trend that will pass
• Maintaining a courteous, helpful and well-organised approach for everyone who has contact with the service	• A frivolous activity only useful to influence consumer spending on food etc
• Creating a welcoming, attractive physical environment	
• Effective communication including developing well-produced, accessible written material	• Unnecessary in an organisation providing a service
A set of attitudes and techniques designed to **evaluate** what you do and how you do it so that it can be done more **effectively**	IRRELEVANT TO DEVELOPING BEST PRACTICE
PROVIDING AN EFFICIENT, EASY-TO-USE SERVICE	

yet, if the language is by, and for, professionals, large sectors of the target population may 'switch off'.

Clark *et al* (1995) explain how the NHS reforms have 'ushered in a whole new vocabulary' which has rapidly been adopted by those concerned with health care provision. They quote the Hunter *et al* (1994) list of concepts which need to be understood by health care professionals: managed competition, internal markets, purchaser/provider separation, diversification of supply to include the voluntary and private sectors, health gain, regulation and consumerism.

Box 8 – Language Dilemmas

There is a need to **describe** your aims and outcomes to a wide range of people including:

◆   purchasers

◆   patients/clients/relatives/carers

◆   other nurses

◆   other health care workers

Each group uses different terms. The challenge is to use the appropriate terminology to ensure effective communication, for example:

PURCHASERS MIGHT USE	NURSING COLLEAGUES MIGHT USE
• performance indicators	• holistic care
• outcomes	• therapeutic management
• audits	• reflective practice
• targeted services	• self care
• increased uptake of services	• individualised care

The goal is the same – to share knowledge and experience – the words used are:
TARGETED FOR A SPECIFIC AUDIENCE

Developing communication skills

Spontaneous comments about the value of a communications workshop, held at the King's Fund, emerged from members of the focus group. This session had been motivating and worthwhile, offering insights and advice on how to proceed as professionals who wanted to publicise what they were doing. Drawing on communications expertise had opened up a range of new possibilities, as outlined in Box 9 on page 10.

Box 9 – The Communication Workshop

A one-day session of advice and discussion on effective communication had been held for clinical leaders of NDUs. Four years on, the workshop, which was facilitated by a professional communications expert, was warmly remembered by group participants as having stimulated them to view their work quite differently.

The course aims were to:

◆ discuss communication challenges facing NDUs;

◆ become familiar with procedures for dealing with the media;

◆ consider options for local printed publicity.

The course content was:

◆ dealing with the media;

◆ communication challenges;

◆ with whom do we want to communicate?

◆ maintaining a high profile for NDUs.

There is some very useful literature available on developing skills to communicate effectively, which may be drawn on by practitioners keen to develop in this way. The example in Box 10 illustrates one strategy for use by those wanting to enhance the effectiveness of their negotiations with others.

Box 10 – Seven Key Stages in Approaching Negotiations

◆ Define goals and objectives

◆ Clarify the issues

◆ Gather information

◆ Humanise and set the climate

◆ Prepare for conflict

◆ Prepare for compromise and resolution of the issues

◆ Prepare for agreement and confirmation

Source: Maddux (1988)

Fisher *et al* (1991) write of 'principled negotiation' – a series of guidelines for dealing with potentially fraught working relationships. Their suggestions include:

- playing a more active role in the purchasing process;
- separating the people (with whom you are negotiating) from the problem;
- focusing on the best outcomes rather than any entrenched 'positions' – all players are interested in the best possible service for users;
- seeking options for *mutual* gain and not 'win or lose';
- establishing objective criteria to aid decision-making.

Providers are reminded that negotiations are two-sided and that 'you have something they want' – the ability to provide a good service, a responsiveness to users and the community, flexibility and value for money – and urge them to 'hold on to your strengths'.

Similarly, Maddux (1988) emphasises the need to think through the issues, to identify what is important and why, so that you can present your views to the other party in a way that helps them to understand what you are saying. Trying to identify priorities for the other party and how they are likely to respond should facilitate constructive discussions. Maddux suggests that this work on identifying issues should be followed by finding out about the people with whom you will be negotiating, and the practical details of the negotiating process.

Information and anecdotes

The group participants discussed the use of anecdotes and case histories in the process of negotiating with decision-makers. Having prepared carefully for meetings or presentations to which they had been called, they had the relevant statistical information available in detailed reports about what they were seeking to promote. While not suggesting that anecdotes or the experiences of individuals could form the basis for a debate, it was clear that sometimes they helped to force a point home or to make concrete something of which the decision-makers may have had no experience. One participant, for example, had prepared a paper on pressure sore prevention and the strategies she and her colleagues were proposing for community nursing. Their points and concerns had been accepted, but it was felt that their photographic evidence of pressure sores had been extremely influential in gaining the attention of the planners.

Looking outwards

Group participants were clear about how nursing needed to utilise its 'marketable' qualities and some of these suggestions are outlined in Box 11. There needed to be a systematic 'tuning-in' to how nurses could play a full part in the system in which they worked. By routinely noting their positive outcomes, nurses could be sending a much more coherent message about their work. Similarly, finding out about parts of the system that related to their work could significantly influence how much of a contribution nurses made. For example, focus group members felt that it was possible to ask for straightforward information about the relevant parts of a complex, organisational framework, such as financing. These and other strategies are outlined in Box 12.

BOX 11 – MARKETING STRATEGIES

Group participants identified ways in which they and their colleagues could market nursing more effectively:

◆ Capitalise on positive outcomes/features of best practice.

◆ Network effectively with all who have a stake in practice and its development.

◆ Establish channels of communication to inform all who need to know about the work of nurses and the successes. Resist the professional 'pat on the back' that goes no further.

◆ Remember that many people are in hospital because it is *nursing* they need, and make the voice of nursing heard.

◆ Develop an awareness and understanding of the parts of the structure and the procedures that directly affect your work. It is not necessary to be aware of the whole accounting structure of the organisation for which you work, for example, but it is **essential** to be familiar with the part of that structure that impacts on your practice.

◆ See your work as part of a strategic plan for providing the best possible care so that you are not simply reacting to requests and demands.

◆ Set your workplace development in the context of your organisation's objectives and with an awareness of purchasers' priorities and plans.

The group members varied in how much contact they had had with purchasers and how appropriate it would be for them to have such contact in their current post. The locality manager was in the most direct regular contact with purchasers and the clinical leader, in a unit funded by extra contractual referrals (ECRs)[2] was also more involved with purchasers than would generally be the case. For some of the group members, knowing more about who the purchasers were and how they operate would have been helpful. What group members had in common was a desire to know about the structures that had an impact on how they worked, and to take all the opportunities they could to market their unit and develop its potential. This was not an elite that had worked though the process, but a group that wanted to be well-informed and innovative.

Participants' discussions of their marketing experience linked with a broad notion of looking out beyond the immediate working environment and relating to others about the practice in which you are engaged and the structures in which you work. The key elements of these are presented in Box 12.

BOX 12 – WORKING WITH OTHERS

PRACTICE

Having contact with:

- nurses
- others

STRUCTURES

Understanding:

- financial arrangements
- purchaser–provider systems
- constraints on all key players
- where immediate practice fits into the organisation

PROCEDURES

Knowing about:

- the organisation's objectives
- priorities, strengths and limitations
- the consultative and decision-making procedures
- developing effective channels of communication

---

2. These are referrals to provider units which do not have a core contract with the purchaser.

Group participants varied in the openness and supportiveness of the working environment of which they were part. Some of them were in direct contact with purchasers because of the role they had or the way their provision was organised. What was clear, however, was that all were interested in maintaining an informed presence and in being able to lead junior colleagues to an understanding of their wider responsibilities to marketing, etc. An example of this is presented in Box 13.

Box 13

Staff in one unit were uneasy about the activity targets set for them for the coming year and were concerned about the high level of corporate overheads operating in their organisation. They saw the targets as having been imposed on them arbitrarily by 'management'. The clinical leader had, in fact, been involved in setting them as part of the negotiations for developing provision. These discussions had focused on how to ensure that the service was cost-effective, yet maintained quality standards and the capacity for staff support and development. It had been important here to emphasise to staff that they had been represented in these negotiations and that their service did not exist in a vacuum. An awareness of the connections between activity targets and the cost of providing the service and of the relationship between price and market-ability was essential if they were to understand, and respond to, the context in which they worked.

Where lines of management *were* clear and supportive, group participants were invited to contribute to business plans etc., but frequently information was all one-way. Some did not know *to what* they were contributing, neither did they feel they received sufficient feedback. They would like to have felt part of the wider structure, rather than simply to have been transmitters of information about their unit.

Group participants felt that practitioners sometimes became embroiled in the negative, frustrating aspects of their work and lost sight of the many positive outcomes they secured. This need to emphasise achievements and effective practice was not always recognised. A massage service for patients receiving radiotherapy could be presented, for example, in terms of its proposed outcomes and its potential for prevention. Such a service could:

- ease the pain and discomfort for patients after treatment;
- decrease the chances of re-admission as an in-patient;
- shorten the length of stay in hospital by speeding up the recovery process.

Linking such strategies with a business approach suggests ways in which practitioners can influence the contracting process appropriately, as outlined in Box 14.

BOX 14 – EFFECTIVE CONTRACT MANAGER

◆ Your business plan makes it clear that you know what you are doing as professional carers.

◆ You have the means of ensuring that the quality of service to your clients is appropriate to their needs.

◆ You have ways of monitoring that it remains so.

◆ Services are offering value for money and the costs have been thought through.

◆ You have an appropriate and effective management structure.

◆ You can demonstrate a commitment to staff and to developing their skills and competence.

◆ You have information systems to tell purchasers how all these things are working.

Source: Dutfield (1993)

Box 15 overleaf illustrates the need to capitalise on positive outcomes. An approach to work that was alert to marketing would have ensured that this positive message was used constructively. The calls for evidence-based practice (GB Welsh Office, 1995 and Vaughan and Edwards, 1995) illustrate the importance being attached to the recording and dissemination of such outcomes. In the same vein, Marsh and Macalpine (1995) report that 'the key theme that emerged for nurse managers was naming and recognising their value'. The need for a different approach to 'publicity' is highlighted by the SNMAC[3] (1995) who feel that: 'Family health visitors have been too reticent about the promotional and preventive value of what they do, and often overlook rigorous evaluation of the innovative solutions to problems they have detected'.

---

3. Standing Nursing Midwifery Advisory Committee.

Box 15

Two surveys, conducted four years apart, by the Community Health Council in the town served by a large maternity unit had suggested a decrease in post-delivery pain and discomfort for local women. This decrease coincided with midwives taking a more extended role in the suturing of women following childbirth. This potential 'boost' for the development of midwifery practice had not been capitalised upon, or publicised to anyone outside the immediate practice environment.

As shown in Box 16, the role of practitioners is sub-divided into two approaches: pro-active and re-active. The first is about looking outwards routinely and capitalising on opportunities. It relates to Marsh and Macalpine's point (1995) about the increasing importance of practitioners asking: 'How else could we do this?' The second is concerned with responding to the views and reactions of others. *Both* have a key role to play in the development of a responsive practice base.

Box 16

PRO-ACTIVE

◆ Identify gaps

◆ Take steps to meet them

◆ 'Sell' to managers and purchasers

e.g. Nurses working in oncology had large numbers of patients with lymphoedema for whom they had no specialist service. Having identified a need they undertook the appropriate training to develop the service and gained the necessary competences. Specific support for those patients has now become an integrated part of this unit's provision.

RE-ACTIVE

◆ Changing or ceasing service

e.g. A team of health visitors recognised a need to respond more effectively to the needs of their local population and revised their staffing structure to allow one colleague to work exclusively on public health work. This specialist post had enhanced the service's responsiveness to clients and its involvement in multi-agency work.

◆ Starting new work in response to 'customers'

e.g. When a patients' forum was introduced, staff working with elderly people were made aware that clients were reluctant to use the garden due to anxieties about not being able to contact staff should they need to. Knowing of these concerns, staff negotiated with managers to extend the call-bell system so that it could be used from the garden area. This meant that clients could benefit more fully from the outdoor amenities available to them.

Working with GPs, to take another example, could mean the development of a shared understanding, as was the case in the community nursing service already discussed; alternatively, it could refer to developing collaborative working practices and channels for communication. One of the group participants reported that her unit's contact with GPs had highlighted the vast amount of documentation the latter received. The unit had therefore made strenuous efforts to provide an accessible, responsive system that GPs could access. GPs were visited, given written information about the unit, and telephone calls and enquiries were dealt with efficiently. The presentation of the unit was seen as crucial to ensuring its place in health care provision. As one participant explained: 'You could offer the most brilliant service [to clients] and if the GP doesn't know, so what?'

Public images

How the service appears to outsiders and the image it conveys has implications beyond the nurses involved. The receptionist, for example, will be most people's first contact with the health centre and how the initial conversations with him or her are received will influence how provision is seen. All the administration and clerical staff need to be aware of the importance of their response to callers and visitors, and of the part they have to play in creating the public image of the service.

The group participants were also accustomed to requests to visit their workplaces and they had developed strategies to manage these demands. One effective system was to decide on dates for visits well in advance, advertise them in the nursing press and then give these dates to any enquirers. This limited the disruption to work and yet gave a positive response to those who were interested in the unit's practice. In some instances, visitors were charged a nominal sum of £10 to cover costs (for example of photocopied articles or refreshments).

This need to look beyond the immediate demands of the working environment can be extremely stressful, and balancing competing pressures was a persistent theme in the focus group. Identifying a specialist niche was an extra responsibility and it was difficult to judge when to invest time and energy for a potential gain in the longer term. If managers were unable to support an initiative at the early stages, it was difficult for practitioners to decide whether to extend their work or to wait for support that may not be forthcoming anyway. This need to be 'visionary' was new to most practitioners and group members emphasised the need for support and effective teamwork if they were to take it on. It required a commitment to planning for the immediate working area that was pro-active and well-informed. An illustration of how this shift had taken place was reported in the group, where members of one practice unit move up a grade if they are able to generate the appropriate level of funding.

Training

Group participants were clear that training was essential if practitioners were to utilise fully the opportunities marketing presented. There was a consensus that there should be *some* coverage of this topic in pre-registration courses to alert students to the fact that this approach should be part of their work. It was agreed, however, that pre-qualifying nurses were unlikely to have sufficient understanding of what nursing entailed and its possibilities really to grasp the marketing points. It was post-registration work that provided realistic opportunities to develop nurses' awareness and skills.

Practising nurses need to be conscious that marketing has real potential for developing their work and there was optimism that, as more people in senior posts acknowledge the importance of maintaining nursing's profile, less-experienced colleagues would be able to follow their example. This was not just seen as giving people skills, but was a measure to encourage a climate where the patient is the priority and nursing carefully monitoring, evaluating, and refining practice to become as efficient and effective as possible.

Measuring progress

Moving on to monitoring, a marketing approach to organising data collection and analysis can reap great rewards. The resulting information can be used to evaluate quality and performance to professional standards. Some pertinent questions that apply to both marketing and quality assurance are listed in Box 17.

BOX 17 – MONITORING PERFORMANCE

◆ What services are being provided?

◆ What needs are services expected to meet?

◆ How is meeting needs measured?

◆ What are the optimum levels of performance and quality?

◆ How are changing needs monitored and necessary adjustments made?

◆ Are those involved able to reflect on their practice and the organisation they work for in a constructively critical way?

A PROCESS OF COLLECTING INFORMATION THAT CAN BE USED TO EVALUATE QUALITY AND PERFORMANCE

Frustrations/constraints

While there was a strong commitment among group participants to taking on the broad role outlined in this report, they were sometimes aware that the system in which they worked had not absorbed the change. Participants spoke fully, for example, of the efforts they had made to publicise their work. Such activities made considerable demands on practitioners who would not necessarily have the experience or training to prepare conference papers or articles. Participants were clear however that such activities had been worthwhile. Those involved had gained in confidence from this wider context and had valued seeing how their work compared with that being undertaken elsewhere.

Seeing the personal and professional growth of colleagues who had not previously taken part in these activities had been rewarding, although the sometimes rather 'picky' requirements of conference paperwork, for example, had caused some problems. The frustrations that going outside one's main role can cause was conveyed by one group participant who, having made considerable effort to involve colleagues in developing presentation skills and the confidence to promote their work in this way, had felt unsupported by senior management who had focused on the fact that people were absent from the work-force, rather than on the valuable part they were playing at a conference.

It was agreed by group members that the reward system within nursing needs to adapt if these public presentations are to become part of nursing's remit.

The main areas identified are listed in Box 18 overleaf.

Box 18

Barriers and frustrations were identified that made this new role extremely demanding. While the emphasis throughout was on *solutions* not *problems*, the difficulties encountered need to be acknowledged. These included:

◆ Decisions having to take into account financial considerations so that the preparation and marketing in which the nurses engaged reflected this area of decision making.

◆ The need for nurses to clarify the ways in which they can impact on health care decision makers.

◆ Having to keep up the marketing momentum and not being discouraged. As one clinical leader explained, ten responses to a mailshot of 100 may seem disheartening but it means steady progress in the right direction!

◆ Judging *when* to innovate so that staff did not feel they had wasted their time and had no chance of further support, or that they were unable to be creative and develop their practice.

◆ Balancing these 'extra' activities with the pressing demands of the job to achieve a workable compromise.

Features the group discussed included:

◆ setting realistic time-scales for achieving goals;

◆ self-discipline;

◆ recognising that there are times when activities extend beyond the working week;

◆ the liberating impact of having a stake/influence in your own working environment.

Having outlined why marketing is relevant and some of the ways in which it may be tackled, this section ends with a number of the main points to be considered by practitioners who wish to develop their work in this way. Structural changes or shifts in attitude may be initiated and sustained by key individuals, sometimes working in isolation. The limitations of this 'hero-innovator' approach (*Georgiades and Phillimore, 1975*) are clear, both from the organisation's and the individual's point of view. Some strategies to help balance out the load are listed in Box 19.

Box 19 – Making Change Manageable and Do-able

◆ Delegating – utilising clerical support and relevant expertise, for example marketing, the preparation of publicity materials.

◆ Exploring a range of resources to finance the support, for example one NDU took a multi-agency approach to promote healthy eating, in collaboration with a local supermarket. Similarly, where NHS Trusts have facilities for preparing presentations, publicity and marketing these are generally a cost-effective way of bringing the NDU's work to the attention of a range of people.

◆ Supporting colleagues to broaden their role, for example preparing conference papers.

◆ Developing a climate that supports and encourages innovation so that a range of colleagues feels able to take on new challenges.

BASICALLY – AVOIDING PERSONAL OVERLOAD, BUT MAKING STEADY PROGRESS TOWARDS YOUR GOAL!

References

1. Adirondach, S. and Macfarlane, R. *Getting Ready for Contracts – a guide for voluntary organisations*. London: Directory of Social Change, 1990.

2. Appleby, J. *Developing Contracting – a national survey of district health authorities, boards and NHS trusts*. Birmingham: NAHAT/HSMC University of Birmingham, 1994.

3. Bryant, J. *The professional nursing contribution to purchasing: a study by the King's Fund College*. Leeds: National Health Service Management Executive, 1993.

4. Clark, D, Neale, B, Heather, P. 'Contracting for Palliative Care'. *Social Science Medicine*, 40, 9 (1995) 1193–1202.

5. Dutfield, M. *Effective Contract Management – a guide for care providers*. Birmingham: Pepar Publications, 1993.

6. Fisher, R, Ury, W, Patton, B. *Getting to Yes: negotiating an agreement without giving in*. London: Business Books, 1991.

7. Georgiades, N.J, Phillimore, L. 'The myth of the hero-innovator and alternative strategies for organisational change'; in Kiernan, C.C. & Woodford, F.P. (eds) *Behavioural Modification and the Severely Retarded*. New York: Associated Scientific Publications, 1975.

8. Great Britain Department of Health, *National Health Service and Community Care Act*. London: HMSO, 1990 (Chapter 19).

9. Great Britain Department of Health, *Targeting Practice – the Contribution of Nurses, Midwives and Health Visitors*. London: Department of Health, 1993

10. Great Britain National Health Service Executive. *Developing NHS Purchasing and GP Fundholding. Towards a Primary Care-Led Service EL(94)79*. Leeds: Department of Health, 1994

11. Great Britain The Welsh Office. *Towards Evidence-based Practice – a clinical effectiveness initiative for Wales*. Cardiff: The Welsh Office, 1995.

12. Ham, C. *Management and Competition in the new NHS*. Abingdon: Radcliffe Medical Press, 1994.

13, Holliday, I. *The NHS Transformed – a Guide to the Health Reforms*. Manchester: Baseline Books, 1995.

14. Howard, E, Hublebank, J, Moore, P. 'Employer evaluation of graduates: use of the group.' *Nurse Educator*, 14, 5 (1989) 38–41.

15. Hunter, D., Colling, C, Green, A. 'Why the world should be wary'. *The Guardian*, 9 March 1994.

16. Jowett, S. 'Review: Focus group interviews in nursing research.' *Nursing Times Research*, 1, 2 (1996) 154–5.

17. Macleod Clark, J, Maben, J, Jones, K. 'The use of focus group interviews in nursing research: Issues and challenges'. *Nursing Times Research*, 1, 2 (1996) 143–53.

18. Maddux, R.B. *Successful Negotiation*. London: Kogan Page, 1988

19. Marsh, S, Macalpine, M. *Our Own Capabilities – clinical nurse managers taking a strategic approach to service improvement*. London: King's Fund Publishing, 1995.

20. Nyamathii, A, Schuler, P. 'Focus group interview: A research technique for informed nursing practice', *Journal of Advanced Nursing*, 15 (1990) 1281–8.

21. (SNMAC) Report of the Standing Nursing and Midwifery Advisory Committee. *Making it happen. Public Health – the contribution, role and development of nurses, midwives and health visitors*. Leeds: Department of Health, 1995.

22. Vaughan, B, Edwards, M. *Interface between Research and Practice – some working models*. London: King's Fund Centre, 1995.

23. Yorkshire RHA/Greenhalgh and Company. *Using Information in Contracting. Module 4 – Setting NHS Contracts*. Macclesfield: Greenhalgh & Company Ltd, 1993.

Appendix 1

Purchasers and providers

The internal market reforms in the NHS were introduced in the National Health Service and Community Care Act (GB. DOH, 1990). They were operationalised in stages from April 1991. The key feature of the reforms is the separation of purchasers from providers. The simplest relationship is between one purchaser and one provider. From April 1996, all District Health Authorities (DHAs) and Family Health Service Authorities (FHSAs) merged into Health Authorities (HAs) to form integrated purchasing organisations.

The basic components of the purchasing structure are listed below:

- an HA purchasing and an NHS Trust providing;

- a General Practitioner Fund Holder (GPFH) purchasing and an NHS Trust providing.

In practice, arrangements are frequently more complex as purchasers and providers form collaborative groupings. For purchasers this could include:

- a consortium of GPFHs;

- a consortium of HAs;

- an HA and the Local Authority (LA);

- an HA and GPFHs.

For providers this could include:

- a hospital and community provider;

- an NHS provider and voluntary services;

- an NHS provider and the private sector;

- two separate hospital providers;

- an NHS provider and social services.

More complex arrangements exist when a provider also acts as a purchaser. A provider may buy from another to comply with a contract held with a purchaser.

GP fund-holders

GPFHs control their own budget and both provide and buy some health care. A fund-holding GP can select secondary patient care, instead of relying on purchasing decisions made by another body. The size of practice eligible for fund-holding status has fallen from 11,000 patients (April 1991) to 5,000 (April 1996). In April 1995, 10,410 GPs in 2,603 practices, covering 41 per cent of the population, were GPFHs (*Holliday, 1995*).

Since April 1996 three types of fund-holding have been in operation:

- standard fundholding (reduced minimum of 5,000 patients to qualify);

- community fundholding (minimum of 3,000 patients – able to purchase restricted range of community services);

- total fundholding (control over almost all purchasing decisions).

Appendix 2

Purchaser–provider contracts

Contracts specify the cost, quality and quantity of care to be provided. They are produced at the end of the purchasing process and they set down in writing the range of services that providers have agreed to deliver. They are the product of at least two key decision-makers and they set out what both must do. Even though, in most cases, they are not legally binding, considerable care needs to be exercised in thinking through the implications of what is recorded on paper.

◆ **Background**

- details of the parties involved

- date and duration of contract

- name of authorised officer (purchasing)

- name of contracting officer (providing)

◆ **Service specifications**

- the organisation's aims

- a description of the service

- the objectives of the service

- where the service will be located and when delivered

- for whom it will be available

- fees and method of payment (if applicable)

- how the services relate to the overall executive plan

- options re sub-contracting and who would manage such a workforce

◆ **Service standards**

- standard of service to be provided

- criteria for assessment of service

- user involvement

- complaints procedures

- criteria for sections/referral of patients/clients

- assessment and review of users

- system for discharge

◆ **Equal opportunities**

- procedures for ensuring fair access

- equal opportunities monitoring

◆ **Shared responsibilities**

- statements about which decisions purchasers will be expected to be consulted, for example referrals, or which will be for providers only

- procedures for consultation and dispute resolution

◆ **Monitoring and evaluation**

- liaison group to oversee/advise on services provided under the contract

- how services will be assessed and by whom

- how frequently monitoring reports will be produced and what they should cover

- other monitoring tools – periodic inspections, surveys of users, independent assessments, procedures for negotiating changes in services due to changing needs or demand

It is crucial when commissioning services to establish quality standards agreed by the purchasers and the provider, and informed by the needs of users. Purchasing authorities need to build quality standards into each phase of the purchasing cycle in consultation with the providers.

♦ **Quality criteria**

- effectiveness (achieving the intended benefits of intervention)

- acceptability and humanity (to both service user and provider)

- equity and accessibility (availability to all)

- efficiency (the avoidance of waste)

- appropriateness (tailoring services to need)

♦ **Financial**

- cost and payment method

- basis for payment – block, *per capita*, cost per volume

- the cost of the service in the previous year (if applicable)

- management costs (preparatory and continuing)

- timing of staged payments

- conditions for payment

- frequency and content of financial reports by provider to purchaser

- procedures for reviewing and varying unforeseen costs

◆ **Staffing**

- number of staff and staff ratios

- staffing grades and structure

- selection and recruitment and purchaser's role

- terms and conditions of employment

◆ **Review and variation**

- frequency and process of scheduled reviews

- procedures for altering/varying contracts – dealing with unexpected changes in needs or costs

- response if there is a breach of contract or non-payment of monies due

Appendix 3

Producing contracts

In this section the types of contract are outlined, some trends in contracting are listed and the cycle for producing contracts is itemised. The appendix ends with some points about the negotiating process.

Types of contract

As the contracting process has developed, variations on these broad groupings have evolved.

TYPES OF CONTRACT	
Block	a block contract for a whole service
Block with ceilings and floors activity/spending	agreed sum of money over a year to deliver a defined range of services, e.g accident and emergency provision to a local population
Cost and volume	agreed price for a specified volume of work – how many patients/clients are to be seen
Cost per case	prices for the treatment of individuals

Trends in contracting

There have been shifts in the number of types of contract (*Appleby, 1994*). The overall number has increased each year, particularly in 1993/4 when they rose from around 1,200 to 3,200. For types of contract, in 1992/3 – 56 per cent were block contracts and in 1994/5, this had fallen to just under 30 per cent with cost per case and block contracts with ceilings and floors covering 28 per cent and 25 per cent respectively. Other trends to note in relation to contracts were:

- Although there has been an increase in cost per case contracts in recent years, spending has halved on this type of contract from £16 million to just under £8 million.

- The value of block contracts has also fallen by more than a half.

- Spending on block contracts with floors and ceiling has risen by over 60 per cent.

- Spending on cost and volume contracts has risen by 14 per cent.

- Appleby *et al* (1994) describe changes in the type of contract agreed between Districts and their providers. The move is towards more sophisticated forms with greater attention being paid to the analysis of the financial and other risks involved.

- There may be moves away from a 'contract currency' (*Ham, 1994*) for a whole service or patient group to packages of care which can cut across traditional definitions of specialties.

The cycle for producing contracts

- Purchasers undertake a need assessment and determine their purchasing strategy.

- They decide and describe their objectives for meeting the health needs of their population and the types of service they want to purchase to meet them.

- These are written down in a Commissioning Plan or Purchasing Intentions that determine service specifications (setting overall strategies, priorities and targets for service development).

- One or more providers identify how they can meet the purchaser's objectives and the costs of that provision.

- Purchasers and providers clarify the situation – focusing on the service being delivered, its quality and costs.

- Purchasers decide which combination of services they wish to buy and from whom.

- Purchasers establish procedures to monitor services to ensure quality and value.

TWO 'CONFOUNDING FACTORS'

◆   Information required is often incomplete or inadequate.

◆   Time, effort and/or expertise required is not always available.

Source: Yorkshire RHA/Greenhalgh and Company Ltd (1993)

Negotiating contracts

SEEING THE PURCHASERS' PERSPECTIVE

◆   What do they really want from this specific contract?

◆   What do they see as the needs of these particular clients?

◆   Which of the many possible deciding factors are most important for them at this time?

The number and content of meetings required to decide on a final contract varies considerably. In some instances, a small number of staff from purchasing and providing will meet once or twice to secure a workable arrangement. On other occasions a series of meetings, drawing in senior personnel, will be required to reach a satisfactory outcome.

Staff potentially included in the negotiating process:

PROVIDERS	PURCHASERS
Chief Executives	General Practitioners and their Fund Managers
Clinical Directors	District General Managers
Medical Officers	Directors of Finance
Directors of Contracting	Health Commission Managers
Directors of Quality	Directors of Contracting
Unit Accountants	Directors of Quality
Directors of Nursing	Directors of Information/Planning
Directors of Information	

Features of negotiation

These include:

◆ There is discussion of a range of issues – not just price or any one other dominant issue.

◆ It should examine qualitative and quantitative aspects of service delivery. In practice, price – or contract value – has proved to be a major issue (*Yorkshire RHA/Greenhalgh and Company Ltd, 1993*).

◆ Careful preparation is required.
   This includes obtaining and absorbing information about:

   • the other 'side';

   • your own organisation;

   • the procedures and practice of negotiation.

Facts that providers should know about purchasers:

- the value and volume of contracts made by them (current and previous year)

- the purchasers' actual (and potential) budget;

- the contingency reserves held in the previous year;

- the intended contingency reserves;

- the purchasers' priorities;

- the number of extra contractual referrals (ECRs) in the previous year;

- the offers available from other providers (if applicable)

As explained (*Yorkshire RHA/Greenhalgh and Company Ltd, 1993*), much of this information should be relatively easy to obtain, as it is in the public domain. Sources will include: the commissioning plan, statistical returns and previous contracts.

Data collection and analysis

Background information

Prior to the focus group meeting, a series of telephone contacts was made. Each of the 13 practitioners invited to the session was asked to provide brief details of their work environment and their suggestions for topics for the focus group. In addition, telephone calls were made to a variety of senior personnel, – both purchasers and providers – mainly from a nursing background, to discuss key issues for exploration. A list of issues generated from this process was sent to all those who would be attending, prior to the session. These direct contacts were supplemented by a review of some relevant literature.

The focus group

Sandra Jowett suggested topics to be covered during the meeting and Barbara Vaughan participated in the discussion, contributing her detailed knowledge of the work in which participants were engaged

As Macleod Clark et al (1996) explain, focus group interviews are being utilised increasingly in nursing research. Their paper is recommended (*Jowett, 1996*) for its 'detailed description of how the research was planned and conducted and in the guidance it offers to others wishing to use this method'. A focus group was used in this study, given that the aim was to generate information about how experienced nurse practitioners had engaged in marketing practices and how they felt nurses could and should develop this aspect of their work.

The focus group technique is described by Howard et al (1989) as being 'simply a discussion in which a small group of people under the guidance of a facilitator or moderator, talk about topics selected for investigation. Participants answer the questions posed by the moderator, make comments, ask questions of other participants and respond to other participants' questions'. The comment by Macleod Clark et al (1996) that 'they are a form of group interview that capitalises on communication between research participants in order to generate data' highlights the strength of the approach undertaken for this study in that the points raised were reflected upon and clarified by group members.

The session ran between 10am and 4pm starting with an informal discussion over coffee and including a short break for lunch approximately mid-way. Further 'comfort' breaks were taken as appropriate. Apart from these break times the whole session was tape-recorded and notes of key points were hand-written throughout. Key areas for discussion were listed on a flipchart prior to the session, with further comments added as the group progressed.

The group was loosely structured with the following five broad sections:

1. Welcome and introductions

2. Open discussion

3. Reference to the points listed on the flip chart

4. Summing-up and opportunities for clarification

5. Expression of thanks to participants.

The open discussion section was particularly fruitful given that the participants had already spoken to the facilitator about the work they were engaged in and were aware of the purpose and aims of the group. As explained, a list of issues had been sent to participants prior to the group – a list generated partly through the telephone contact with them. The group discussion was lively and fast-moving, although all participants took time to listen to the contributions of others and incorporated them into their own response. Where there was discord, this was handled constructively and honestly and differing views and experiences were respected.

Analysis

The author used three sources of information from the group to write this report – the tape-recording, the notes made during the discussion and the headings written on the flip charts and added to during the session. The tape was listened to carefully noting down the key themes and points to emerge and working details of them as they emerged. The information gleaned from the tapes was then supplemented by that from the chart and notes. The examples from practice were drafted as they arose on the tape and then slotted into the appropriate place in the report. Once the main theme to be addressed in each of the boxes had been identified, other points were collated within those groupings.

Appendix 5

Focus group participants

Christine Halek
Annex NDU

Karen Iley
Byron NDU

Sue Lowson
Southampton NDU

Sue Mason
Glenfield NDU

Janet Sheard
Strelley NDU

Sandra Jowett
National Foundation for Educational Research (now working at Public Attitude
Surveys, High Wycombe)

Barbara Vaughan
King's Fund